Cosens
Pleasure Steamers

ANDREW GLADWELL

AMBERLEY

First published 2013

Amberley Publishing
The Hill, Stroud
Gloucestershire, GL5 4EP

www.amberley-books.com

British Library Cataloguing in Publication Data.
A catalogue record for this book is available from the British Library.

ISBN 978 1 4456 1450 2
E-book ISBN 978 1 4456 1464 9

Typeset in 10pt on 12pt Sabon.
Typesetting and Origination by Amberley Publishing.
Printed in the UK.

Contents

The famous trio of *Embassy*, *Consul* and *Monarch* were well-loved paddle steamers of the Cosens fleet during the sunset of services in the 1950s and 1960s.

Acknowledgements

This book has been written to evoke the heritage and atmosphere of the well-loved paddle steamers that plied their trade to the traditional seaside resorts of Dorset, Hampshire and the Isle of Wight by the famous Cosens fleet. This book intends to remember in particular the final and happy years of the Cosens fleet and their steamers: *Consul*, *Embassy* and *Monarch*. In compiling this book, I have been grateful for the help and cooperation of several individuals. In particular, I would like to thank Chris Jones, Kieran McCarthy, John Hines, Frank Jones, Jean Spells, Simon Fuller, Fred Gilmore and John Franks.

Websites

For further information on the heritage of paddle and pleasure steamers:
www.heritagesteamers.co.uk

For details of the Vintage Excursion Ship Balmoral:
www.mvbalmoral.org.uk

For details of cruises by the pleasure steamer Kingswear Castle:
www.dartmouthrailriver.co.uk

For details of cruises by the pleasure steamers Balmoral and Waverley:
www.waverleyexcursions.co.uk

For details of the Paddle Steamer Preservation Society:
www.paddlesteamers.org.uk

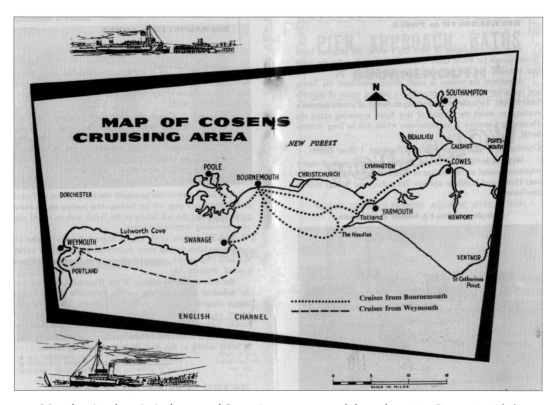

Map showing the principal routes of Cosens' steamers around the early 1960s. Cosens provided a vast number of cruises along the dramatic and beautiful Dorset coast as well as to the Isle of Wight.

Introduction

The well-loved seaside resorts of Dorset were popular destinations and embarkation points for pleasure steamers for over 100 years. For many, the post-Second World War paddle steamer trio, *Monarch*, *Embassy* and *Consul*, provided a fine and nostalgic link back to the past. All three steamers had long and interesting careers and provided the finest way to explore the dramatic coastline of Dorset, Hampshire and the Isle of Wight until services declined in the 1950s and ultimately finished in the mid-1960s.

Cosens' history went back over a century to when Joseph Cosens placed the small paddle steamer *Highland Maid* in service between Weymouth and Portland. She was soon replaced by the larger steamer named *Princess*. The service soon proved to be successful and Captain Cosens developed services and went into partnership with Joseph Drew. They introduced the *Prince* in 1852 and this signalled the expansion of services to places like Poole, Cherbourg and Lulworth Cove. The 1850s and 1860s were typified by competition from other operators that wanted to capture some of the ever-growing tourist market. One new name on the scene was John Tizard, who introduced *Premier* and Bannockburn at Weymouth in 1859. Steam trains arrived at Weymouth in 1857 and with them they bought a great influx of potential passengers for the paddle steamers. This coincided with the construction of the many fine seaside piers that were to provide the perfect calling points for the Cosens fleet in the century that followed.

By the 1870s, the founders of the company had died, but the company was strong and was to see significant growth in the decades that followed. By this time, the company had expanded services and operated to places such as Lyme Regis, Sidmouth and Budleigh Salterton. Services expanded even more when Bournemouth Pier became a main calling point with the construction of the landing facilities that could accommodate four paddle steamers at a time. Bournemouth was developing as a major resort at the time and Cosens were quick to maximise their hold on trade. To show their confidence they placed the *Empress* in service in 1879. The following decade saw an increase in competition from a local company that was keen to take some of the trade with their steamer

Lord Elgin. This inevitably meant that Cosens placed in service larger and better steamers and *Victoria*, *Monarch*, *Queen* and *Albert Victor* entered service.

Queen Victoria's memorable Diamond Jubilee of 1897 was the next catalyst of change. The event was marked by a large number of paddle steamers from other areas of the UK assembling for the review. The success of the event led to other operators wanting a slice of the revenue on the South Coast. With the entry into the arena of P. & A. Campbell, Cosens and Red Funnel needed to react. Cosens did this by placing the *Majestic* in service. She was a large and eminently comfortable paddle steamer and became the flagship of the Cosens fleet when introduced in 1901. Additions to the fleet in the Edwardian era included the *Emperor of India*. This steamer joined at what was undoubtedly the peak of the Cosens business when their fleet was at its most extensive and luxurious and its routes were the most developed.

The boom burst when the First World War started and the Cosens fleet soon took up important wartime roles. At the end of the conflict, the steamers quickly resumed their peacetime role again after refit work. Sadly, Cosens' magnificent flagship *Majestic* had been lost during the conflict. The company reacted by entering a period of calm when no new steamers were placed in service unlike the decades before the First World War. This was a time when motor ships were entering service around the coastline of the UK but Cosens still preferred traditional-looking and generally modest-sized paddle steamers. The interwar years saw Cosens withdraw one of their oldest paddle steamers, the *Premier*, in 1937. She was replaced with the elderly *Duke of Devonshire*, which had been built in 1896 and had been operating in Devon. Cosens renamed her *Consul*. This was swiftly followed by the acquisition of the *Duchess of Norfolk* from the Southern Railway. She was renamed *Embassy*. This interwar flurry of activity took place at a time when people had more leisure time than ever before. When the Second World War started, the Cosens fleet, for the second time in a generation, had its steamers requisitioned for war service. At the end of the conflict, Cosens were fortunate in that none of its paddle steamers had been lost unlike most other operators around the coastline of the UK. With the initial frenzy of demobbed servicemen and civilians wishing to return to their normal peacetime lives, it seemed that the popularity of a paddle-steamer trip on a Cosens steamer would flourish forever. *Victoria* and *Empress* once again took up services from Weymouth, and soon the piers along the South Coast were opened again after work had been undertaken to restore the pier heads to the pier structures. The *Embassy* entered service again in September 1947 and by 1948 the full Cosens fleet was ready again to provide a full service of cruises. *Emperor of India* and *Consul*, like the other steamers in the fleet, underwent refurbishment to make them better equipped for a more modern age.

1946 marked the amalgamation of Cosens with Red Funnel of Southampton. Five years later, another Southern Railway steamer was acquired by Cosens. She was the *Shanklin* and was renamed *Monarch* by Cosens. The early 1950s showed that Cosens had a degree of confidence in the future. Within a couple of years, though, things were changing at a great pace and steamers were withdrawn. Coronation year 1953 saw the venerable *Victoria* withdrawn from the

Cosens fleet and just two years later, the company announced the scrapping of the elderly *Empress*. *Emperor of India* followed just two years later.

By the mid-1950s, the Cosens fleet was severely depleted but it still had three paddle steamers to carry on services, and it was hoped that with a leaner fleet Cosens would be able to carry out cruising along the Dorset coast for many years to come. *Consul*, *Embassy* and *Monarch* became hugely popular in those final years of Cosens. The three steamers had an abundance of character and provided a splendid sunset of cruising along the Dorset coast. The plight of paddle steamers soon became highlighted when the Paddle Steamer Preservation Society was formed in 1959 to try and halt the decline and to preserve the heritage of paddle steamers. As part of this, the PSPS organised charter cruises on *Consul*, *Embassy* and *Monarch*. By the turn of the decade, the Cosens fleet was heading towards its demise. During this time, *Consul* was mainly employed on Weymouth services while *Embassy* and *Monarch* mainly operated from Bournemouth. *Monarch* was the first Cosens steamer to go to the scrapyard in 1961. Price cutting and competition led to a somewhat unsure period of operation. In 1962, and after competition from the *Princess Elizabeth*, *Consul* was withdrawn from service. She did, though, manage a short career elsewhere for other owners. But, she never found success away from the Cosens fleet and was finally scrapped later in the decade. When *Consul* was withdrawn, it was left to *Embassy* to carry on services as the last of the Cosens paddle steamers. She became the last excursion paddle steamer to operate on the South Coast until being withdrawn in 1966 and being sent to the scrapyard. The Cosens' paddle-steamer tradition was now at an end.

By the late 1970s, the paddle steamer *Waverley* made her first visit to the South Coast and visited the old Cosens piers at Weymouth and Bournemouth. The arrival of *Waverley* enabled a new generation, as well as older enthusiasts, to take a nostalgic journey back to the fondly remembered cruises of *Consul*, *Embassy* and *Monarch*. The arrival of the splendid former-South Coast pleasure steamer *Balmoral* in 1986, further increased the interest in cruising along the magnificent Dorset heritage coastline. 2013 saw the arrival of coal-fired paddle steamer *Kingswear Castle* back home on the River Dart. She now provides cruises evocative of Cosens on a river that was known to some of their famous steamers. Now, the pleasure steamers *Balmoral*, *Kingswear Castle* and *Waverley* keep alive the great tradition of pleasure-steamer cruising started by Cosens over a century earlier. By doing so, they enable the present generation to enjoy the simple pleasures of a pleasure steamer that were so beloved of our forefathers on the 'Buff Funnel Fleet'.

Cosens paddle steamers were called up in both wars. *Embassy* is seen here on her return to Weymouth at the end of the Second World War, still in her mine-sweeping livery of battleship grey. (J&C McCutcheon collection)

1

Early Years

Cosens provided paddle-steamer cruises along the Dorset coastline for over a century. One of the most popular destinations for trippers was the beautiful Lulworth Cove. It was the perfect environment for a paddle steamer.

Weymouth from the Nothe

View of Weymouth with *Victoria* alongside the pier. Weymouth developed as a resort during the Georgian era and gained particular popularity when George III visited the town. The fine Georgian hotels that line the esplanade show Weymouth's importance as a seaside resort. It was a natural location for paddle steamers.

Premier departing from Weymouth in atmospheric seas during her heyday. She had an amazingly long career of ninety-one years. She was acquired for Weymouth service by J. Tizard after an early career working on the Clyde between Glasgow and Dumbarton. She had been among the steamers that welcomed Queen Victoria to the Clyde in 1847. Cosens later acquired her for their fleet.

Empress at Lulworth. She had a specially strengthened bow to allow her to land passengers onto the beach at the cove. She was built by Samuda Brothers of Poplar in 1879 – the year of the Zulu War. Cosens' paddle steamers had black-painted funnels until 1901.

Cosens' *Queen* departing from Weymouth with sailors aboard her. Cosens handled the lucrative liberty-boat service to and from nearby Portland.

In 1878, just a few years after she was acquired by Cosens, *Premier* was re-engined and her original steeple machinery was replaced with oscillating engines. Several structural alterations were also made at the time. Further changes occurred in 1885 when she was re-boiled and had her stern replaced.

Helper was part of the Cosens fleet from September 1910 and was acquired in exchange for the *Brodick Castle*. She was well known for ferrying servicemen to Portland. Note the Royal Navy warships at Portland to the right of this view.

Melcombe Regis with Royal Navy warships in the distance. This steamer had a basic layout and limited facilities. This was ideally suited to ferrying servicemen to and from Portland. She was acquired by the company in 1913 after earlier service at Fleetwood and Blackpool.

Premier departing from Weymouth. This steamer originally had a square counter stern but this was later modified to a more curved and softer one. Her early years saw several changes to appearance, but by the late 1880s these were complete.

Albert Victor at sea. This tug was acquired by Cosens in 1888 and had originally been built as *Lass O'Gowrie* in 1883. She was used on tug duties but also saw summer service on local cruises from Weymouth and to Portland.

Passengers Embarking, S.S. " Albert Victor," Weymouth

Above: Edwardian passengers embarking upon the *Albert Victor* at Weymouth Harbour with Nothe Fort in the distance. You can appreciate the open deck in this image and every passenger seems to be wearing the obligatory hat. Cosens were lucky in that they could carry passengers on lucrative short cruises to Lulworth and Portland as well as longer services along the Dorset coast.

Right: Cover for *The Story of Cosens & Company*, published in 1905. This booklet gave a brief summary of the company since it was formed.

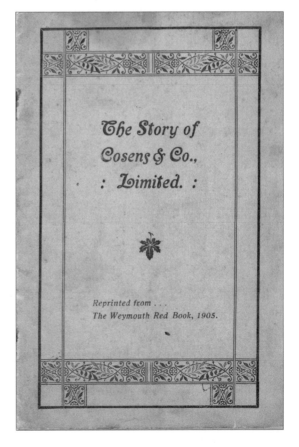

The Story of Cosens & Co., : Limited. :

Reprinted from . . .
The Weymouth Red Book, 1905.

When the First World War ended, the Cosens fleet needed to be restored for their peacetime role. This wasn't an easy thing to achieve as compensation awarded by the government had to be negotiated and the location where the work would be carried out had to be arranged. This could sometimes take many months and years to achieve.

Cosens' Number 2 Slipway at Weymouth, around 1905. The company developed its shipbuilding, engineering and repair facilities at Weymouth. The company purchased many facilities in Weymouth to create an impressive range of buildings where an ever-increasing amount of work could be undertaken.

Above: The wharf outside Cosens' engineering works at Weymouth, around 1905. The company was a major employer in the town. This company continued right up to the 1990s.

Right: A rare view of the fitting shop of Cosens' works at Weymouth around 1905.

Steamer at Landing Stage.

Above: The Dorset coast provided Cosens with an enviable number of calling points including Lulworth Cove. These included the main seaside resorts of Bournemouth, Weymouth and Swanage, as well as short scenic cruises to places such as Lulworth Cove and sightseeing trips to Portland. The company also provided day trips to France during Edwardian times.

Left: Advertisement for Cosens of Weymouth listing the range of their services in 1905. From this list you can appreciate the breadth of their work and their importance to the town.

Passengers disembarking from the *Queen* at Weymouth, around 1910. In the years before the First World War, Cosens offered a wide range of meals and refreshments on their largest steamers. This included luncheons with dishes such as lobster, cold meats and hot joints as well as teas that included tea along with cold meats, lobster or chicken. Cakes, biscuits and bread and butter were also provided along with hot drinks such as cocoa, chocolate, coffee and Bovril.

Cosens' *Empress* during her Dorset-coast heyday. When peace was declared after the First World War, the Cosens fleet was gradually returned by the government. The steamers required a lot of remedial work after extensive wartime use. Cosens recommenced services from Weymouth in 1919. It was to be another two years before the full fleet was once again able to sail.

Empress approaching Weymouth. The loss of the *Titanic* in April 1912 led to life-saving apparatus being upgraded on Cosens' steamers. Some extra lifeboats were added as well as extra lifejackets and buoyant seating. The company also came under more observation to ensure that they operated their steamers safely in conditions such as night-time service.

Cosens was an important element of life at Weymouth. The company was one of the largest businesses as well as providing customers for many hotels, shops and other related businesses connected with the holiday or maritime trade. During the early and mid-nineteenth century, despite being a fashionable and well-established resort, the town was quite remote and had limited access from other towns by road. Travel by sea provided good access to the resort.

Monarch at Alum Bay Pier around 1900. You can see her bell-shaped funnel tops in this view. They were cut off by 1902. The Needles can be seen in the distance.

The pier head at Weymouth. The harbour area had many connections with Cosens. Apart from offices, ship-repair facilities and workshops, there were always the busy queues for the steamers. A common scene at the harbour was the sailors who were ferried to and from Portland Dockyard. Weymouth must have been a lively place at times!

P.S. MONARCH

Monarch was ordered by Cosens in 1888. Her arrival meant that the old *Prince* was offered for sale. The two-funnelled Monarch was built by R. & H. Green of Blackwall in 1888. She was a good steamer for Cosens and was built to enable then to offer cross-Channel services to places such as Cherbourg and Alderney. *Monarch* could carry up to 314 passengers to France and was 210 feet in length. She arrived at Weymouth in June 1888. She was a fine looking steamer with a long elegant saloon on the deck. Passengers were able to walk round this as well as walking upon the roof above it.

Monarch alongside Swanage Pier with *Victoria* departing. The first pier at Swanage was built by John Mowlem in 1859 and was 750 feet in length. It soon became apparent that a larger pier was needed due to an increase in calls by paddle steamers. Work commenced on a new pier in November 1895. The first steamer to call at the new structure was the *Lord Elgin* on 1 May 1896.

Cosens' *Monarch* at the Royal Regatta on the River Dart in Devon. Cosens are best remembered for their services at Weymouth but, at times, they served other areas along the South Coast. *Monarch*'s bridge was relocated in front of her two thin funnels between 1907 and 1908.

Cosens had their home at Weymouth and had seasonal bases at Bournemouth and Swanage during the summer months. The *Monarch* became a minesweeper during the First World War. At the end of the conflict she required a lot of work to recondition her for future service for Cosens.

VIEW FROM THE NOTHE, WEYMOUTH.

Cosens' paddle steamers used the harbour at Weymouth until the Pleasure Pier was built during the interwar years.

Majestic at Bournemouth Pier. *Majestic* operated cruises from Bournemouth and as far east as Brighton. She also operated as far west as Dartmouth during her first season in 1901. In addition, she undertook cruises to Cherbourg.

The elegant bay at Weymouth is known as 'England's Bay of Naples'. The Great Western Railway started a steamer service from Weymouth the Channel Islands in 1857. A few years later in 1865, the railway track was extended to connect with the ferry terminal to form a unique tramway along the quayside. This connected passenger steamers and goods using the port.

The loss of the *Majestic* during the First World War was bad news for Cosens as she was the fastest and largest steamer in the fleet and managed a speed of just over fifteen knots on her trials. *Majestic* could compete with the steamers of rival companies. After the end of the war, Cosens attempted to find a suitable replacement for *Majestic* but in the end decided against replacing the steamer. In the years that followed the conflict, Cosens preferred to acquire old paddle steamers rather than to build new ones.

Brodick Castle around 1908–10. She was built for service to Arran on the Firth of Clyde. She had an extended forecastle and short well deck. Cosens acquired her in 1901. When she arrived on the South Coast, she was one of the largest paddle steamers to be operating.

Brodick Castle departing from a pier during her heyday. Cosens initially operated her from Bournemouth on cruises to the Isle of Wight and Weymouth. In 1908 she moved to Swanage and was disposed of by Cosens shortly after this.

Cosens & Co.'s Steamer "Emperor of India."

Emperor of India was an able and versatile steamer and was 216 feet long and 25 feet wide. She was purchased for the sum of £13,000 by Cosens. At the start of her Cosens career, her master was Captain Tilsed. She had a long and happy link with Bournemouth Pier.

Emperor of India in the Wareham Channel, Poole, after delivery from Thornycroft on 29 January 1908. She was originally going to be called *King Edward VII* but became *Emperor of India* due to the name already being in use.

Emperor of India in her heyday. Her crew are shown in position ready to secure the steamer. *Emperor of India* could carry around 1,390 passengers in calm waters. This was reduced to 481 on cross-Channel routes.

Emperor of India prior to her second reconstruction. After the First World War, the Admiralty stopped the contract to Cosens to provide liberty boats at Portland. The stoppage of this year-round work meant that Cosens then had to withdraw several of their smaller paddle steamers.

Cosens' paddle steamers were one of the most charismatic fleets in the UK. Their distinct atmosphere was centered upon a fleet of steamers that were generally old and traditional. Their pattern of operation also stayed quite static over a century of operation.

2

The Heyday of Cosens

Victoria entering Lulworth Cove. During their heyday, Cosens' steamers operated services right along the spectacular Dorset coast. Short cruises to Lulworth and Portland were always popular and lucrative for the company. Passengers cruising towards Lulworth could admire famous locations along the coastline, such as Kimmeridge.

During the Edwardian era, Bournemouth Pier was becoming incredibly busy and it was clear that more steamers had to be accommodated at the landing stages. New facilities were opened on 5 June 1909. On that day, Cosens' *Majestic* used the new facilities. Note the hats and parasols in this Edwardian view.

Victoria at Lulworth Cove. The first decade or so of the twentieth century is now viewed as the 'Golden Age' of paddle steamers. Cosens experienced a generally good period of operation but it had been one of change and challenges. With the outbreak of the First World War in August 1914, things were to change. Bournemouth Pier reopened to Cosens in 1920. By 1921, the Cosens fleet was complete once again after wartime service.

Premier departing from Bournemouth Pier on 11 July 1936. *Premier*'s withdrawal was announced in 1938. This fine old steamer had served the company for most of its history and had originally been launched in 1846. At the time, she was ninety-two years old and it was said that this small steamer had carried over 2 million passengers during her lifetime. *Premier* was sold for the modest sum of £290 to shipbreakers at Grays.

Victoria in the bay, Weymouth, 1952,. By the mid-1930s, *Victoria*'s future was uncertain due to her age and design. Cosens soon acquired the Southern Railway's steamer *Duchess of Norfolk* for £4,000 and renamed her *Embassy*. *Victoria* was gone a year later, in 1953. (J&C McCutcheon Collection)

Empress at Lulworth Cove. *Empress* was launched in April 1879 and managed a speed of 13 knots in her trials. When she entered service in 1879, one of her initial destinations was to Torquay where she offered cruises.

Hatted passengers aboard the *Alexandra*. In 1932, she was purchased for service on the Thames as the *Showboat*. She offered cabaret for her passengers, who were entertained as they cruised from Westminster Pier. Her funnel was hinged to enable her to go under the London bridges. Stability became a problem and she wasn't a success away from Dorset. She was scrapped at Grays in 1934.

Empress departing from Weymouth. The early 1920s saw Cosens lack a spark. With the decision not to replace *Majestic* with a new large steamer, the company never built a new one again and instead relied on second-hand steamers.

Empress at Lulworth Cove. A calm scene as crew members stand alongside the gangway on the deck and 1930s passengers quietly stroll along the beach. A little bit of *Empress* has survived. The engine of the steamer was restored by apprentices at Southampton Technical College and was then placed on display at Southampton for many years.

Above: A steamer disembarking passengers at Lulworth Cove. *Victoria* was similar looking to *Empress* but was longer and wider. Her paddle box also had wider slats and had a large ventilator in front of the funnel. *Victoria* was also a great deal faster than the *Empress.*

Right: The August 1938 programme of cruises by Cosens from Weymouth. At the time, an extensive programme of cruises was offered. These included trips to Torquay, Bournemouth, Swanage, Yarmouth and Cowes. In addition, a vast number of regular cruises to Lulworth and Portland to view the shipping were included.

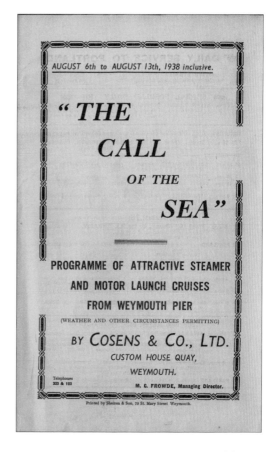

AUGUST 6th to AUGUST 13th, 1938 inclusive.

"THE
CALL
OF THE
SEA"

**PROGRAMME OF ATTRACTIVE STEAMER
AND MOTOR LAUNCH CRUISES
FROM WEYMOUTH PIER**
(WEATHER AND OTHER CIRCUMSTANCES PERMITTING)

BY COSENS & CO., LTD.
CUSTOM HOUSE QUAY,
WEYMOUTH.

Telephones
223 & 123

M. C. FROWDE, Managing Director.

Printed by Sherren & Son, 79 St. Mary Street, Weymouth.

Monarch was re-boilered and had several alterations made to her in 1930. At the end of the
Second World War, after service as an examination vessel, she had further work done to equip
her for her post-war life. She was withdrawn in 1950 and became one of the most reliable and
long-lived paddle steamers of the Cosens fleet. Her splendid bell on its ornate plinth has survived
and is now in the PSPS collection.

Monarch on the slipway at Weymouth. Cosens acquired the slipway at Weymouth during the
mid-1870s and set about making improvements so that they could offer excellent ship-repair
facilities. In 1929, the two-funnelled *Monarch* required significant repairs, and once again
Cosens were wondering whether to repair the steamer or to build a new one. In typical Cosens
style they decided to repair *Monarch* and new boilers were fitted.

Passengers aboard the *Emperor of India* in 1928. The *Emperor of India* saw service in both wars. During the First World War and at the start of the Second World War she undertook minesweeping duties. Towards the end of the Second World War she was used as an anti-aircraft steamer in the Thames Estuary where she served as the flagship of the anti-aircraft flotilla.

Emperor of India was originally built as the *Princess Royal* by Thornycroft at Southampton in 1906 for Red Funnel. The steamer was found to be unsuitable for her new owners and was sold to Cosens in 1908. Cosens renamed her *Emperor of India* and made various alterations. These included lengthening the steamer and extending the topside plating to the bow. They also extended the promenade deck.

Stokers from the *Emperor of India* pose on the sponson around the 1930s at Bournemouth Pier. In the early days, paddle steamers were normally coal-fired. The job of the stoker was a hard one and was made worse by the long hours worked by the steamers during the season. Coaling had to be done after passengers had disembarked.

Emperor of India during her heyday. The mid- to late 1930s was quite a positive period for Cosens. One of the highlights of the decade for the company was the Silver Jubilee Fleet Review at Spithead in 1935 when the Cosens fleet operated trips to take part in the review.

Victoria at Lulworth. The 1920s was a decade of challenges for Cosens. It was a time when national events, such as the General Strike, mixed with poor weather and a depressed economic climate. It was also a decade typified by Cosens making use of their older steamers and not investing in new ones.

Passengers crowd the rails of the *Emperor of India* on 20 May 1937. During that year, members of Cosens' fleet attended the Coronation Fleet Review of George V and Queen Elizabeth. The 1930s was a time of good fortune for Cosens and the refurbished paddle steamers experienced a boom during the brief years between the wars.

Emperor of India during the interwar years. In the mid-1920s, Cosens were once again thinking of having a new and large paddle steamer built. This would enable them to undertake long-distance services. Despite receiving quotes, Cosens once again decided against ordering a new steamer.

Emperor of India approaching Bournemouth Pier. The *Emperor of India* resumed service in 1948 and continued to operate at Bournemouth until the 1956 season. She usually operated the day trips or the double morning and afternoon trips to the Isle of Wight in turn with the *Embassy*.

Happy passengers crowd the decks of the *Emperor of India* at Bournemouth during the interwar years. Less than thirty years later, a scene like this would be history.

The new lifting Town Bridge at Weymouth was opened by HRH the Duke of York in July 1930. The Cosens paddle steamers *Victoria*, *Empress* and *Alexandra* were packed with hundreds of passengers to witness the historic occasion. *Empress* was the first paddle steamer to steam through the new bridge. Cosens' paddle steamers can be seen in the harbour beyond the bridge in this view of the new bridge.

Empress at Lulworth Cove. *Empress* and *Victoria* provided the first post-war trips on 1 June 1946 when they operated local cruises from Weymouth.

By the start of the 1930s, it was decided to rebuild landing facilities at Weymouth. Poor weather, upheaval during building works and uncertainty over facilities made the early 1930s a troubled time for Cosens. To make matters worse, it was also the time of the Great Depression. The harbour improvements were completed at Weymouth in 1933. The new Weymouth Pleasure Pier was a great facility for Cosens and two steamers could be accommodated along its long arm during busy periods.

The cruise to Lulworth Cove was incredibly attractive for Cosens' passengers. It was relatively short, so suited both pockets and the needs of those who could only cope with a short cruise. It also passed many of the most picturesque landmarks of the Dorset coastline, such as Durdle Door and Stair Hole.

Emperor of India tied up at a harbour. Preparations for the Second World War had been planned over a long period and, despite hopes for peace, the country was ready to implement procedures when war was declared on 3 September 1939. Four paddle steamers of the Cosens fleet were immediately placed on examination and contraband services..

Consul at Yarmouth on the Isle of Wight on 22 July 1938. (J&C McCutcheon Collection)

Despite war on the horizon, Cosens were offered the *Queen of Kent* from the New Medway Steam Packet Company fleet but declined the offer. It appeared that this large steamer could have revived day trips to France as the steamer had undertaken such services from Kent. Cosens had more modest intentions for their business.

Duke of Devonshire around 1936 before she was renamed *Consul*. Her first cruise was under the command of Captain Moore who took her from Bournemouth to Swanage.

Consul at Portland on a 'Navy Day' sailing. Note the huge blocks of Portland stone, weighing several tonnes each, ready to be shipped away from the pier. (J&C McCutcheon Collection)

Cosens acquired the *Duke of Devonshire* from her Torquay owner in December 1937. For the 1938 season she was placed on the Portland service instead of the elderly *Premier*. She was renamed *Consul* instead of the first choice of name – *Marquis*.

An early view of *Consul*. *Consul* had several alterations to equip her for her new career with Cosens. The main change was a new funnel that replaced a thinner one. In addition, she had a new mast fitted and her passenger accommodation was improved. *Consul* operated Cosens' final pre-war cruise on 2 September 1939.

Shanklin was renamed *Monarch* in post-war years and became part of the well-loved triplet fleet of *Consul*, *Monarch* and *Embassy*.

Consul laid up at Weymouth in September 1946, having been released from minesweeping duties by the navy, but before her refit for commercial service. (J&C McCutcheon collection)

Three paddle steamers had strong links with Lulworth Cove. *Empress* undertook her final cruise to Lulworth Cove on 9 September 1955. She was scrapped at Southampton soon after. *Victoria* was also often depicted on postcards. *Consul* made two Lulworth Cove sailings one or two days a week in 1961 and was depicted on many postcards.

STEAMER AT LANDING STAGE, LULWORTH COVE.   18048

Empress at Lulworth Cove. By the end of the Second World War, *Empress* was a very old paddle steamer and her days were obviously numbered as part of the Cosens fleet. During her career, she was a very frequent visitor to Lulworth Cove and was depicted on numerous postcards.

A typical view of Lulworth Cove on 8 August 1951. Passengers generally had around an hour ashore at Lulworth. This was enough time to buy an ice cream or souvenir and to have a paddle.

Monarch on the slipway at Weymouth undergoing refit work after the Second World War. Note the painted numbers on the hull indicating plates that needed replacing. After the Second World War, attempts to rebuild the Cosens fleet were hampered by a lack of materials such as timber and steel. Cosens became ingenious in recycling any old materials and fittings that they could find. One such recycling project was the reclamation of wooden panels from Lily Langtry's steam yacht.

The 1949 season looked like being an excellent one for the Cosens fleet. It was blessed with perfect cruising weather and each steamer of the fleet had benefited from post-war refits. Piers had also undergone some degree of rebuilding. Despite the positive tone of the season, the steamers lost money. Blame was placed on the dwindling spending power of passengers as well as competition from other forms of transport. It was a sad indication for Cosens that if they couldn't make a good profit in a season blessed with excellent weather then they would face significant problems if weather was poor or passenger numbers decreased.

Embassy at Weymouth Pleasure Pier. The post-war Cosens fleet was initially a coal-fired one. *Consul*, *Embassy* and *Emperor of India* were later converted to oil-firing.

Victoria approaching Weymouth Pleasure Pier towards the end of her life. She departed Weymouth for the last time on 22 January 1953 for the breakers.

The twin-funnelled *Monarch* had been built for Continental service and could carry over 300 passengers to France. She was also fitted with electric lights. She made her inaugural trip to France on 19 July 1888, taking around five hours from Bournemouth. She could attain a speed of around 16.5 knots. The two-funnelled *Monarch* was an early casualty of the post-war decline and left Weymouth for the final time on 22 February 1950 for the shipbreakers.

Empress in Weymouth Bay. Towards the end of her life she saw stardom in the film *Great Expectations*. Despite being heavily disguised in the film, the film footage has preserved some of the best moving images of a typical Victorian paddle steamer. Cosens disposed of her in 1955.

The entrance to Lulworth Cove could sometimes provide a challenge for masters of Cosens' paddle steamers due to the restricted entrance. This was a particular problem when going astern. The great height of the cliffs surrounding the cove provided a superb opportunity for photographers.

Victoria at Weymouth Pleasure Pier. The withdrawal of *Victoria* at the end of the 1952 season marked the start of the decline of the Cosens fleet. Things were made worse by a lot of poor weather as well as other national and international threats to trading.

Empress at Weymouth. Note her funnel cap and open decks without covered passenger accommodation. She also has that feature that was common among the Cosens steamers – the open bridge. The 1950s witnessed the sharpest decline in the Cosens fleet that had ever been seen, when old Victorian steamers like *Empress* were withdrawn.

Cosens' paddle steamers were an integral part of Weymouth for well over a century. Their steamers could always be seen bringing trippers to and from the town in the summer and were also laid up in the harbour during each winter.

Cosens' steamers alongside Bournemouth Pier. During 1959, Cosens were said to be considering cross-Channel day trips to France and the Channel Islands from Bournemouth.

Steamer at Lulworth Cove. By 1961, the Cosens fleet had, within a decade, shrunk to just two paddle steamers. By this time, the Paddle Steamer Preservation Society had been formed to try and keep alive the memory and tradition of paddle steamers alive. Much of their early work was centered upon the Cosens fleet.

Consul alongside Weymouth Pleasure Pier. 1953 saw Cosens play a major role in the Coronation Fleet Review of Elizabeth II. It took place on 15 June and *Consul*, *Embassy*, *Monarch* and *Emperor of India* undertook a number of cruises for the company to view the assembled fleet. This was the very last time that the South Coast pleasure-steamer fleets were able to show their large fleets. At the end of the event, several of the steamers remained to view the spectacular illuminations and fireworks. The event was a lucrative one for Cosens.

3

Sunset of the Cosens Fleet:
Consul, Embassy & Monarch

Cosens' paddle steamers saw great popularity in the years after the Second World War with the famous steamers *Consul*, *Embassy* and *Monarch*.

Letterhead for Cosens. The style of the letterhead along with its list of previous steamers gives this a dated look. By this time, the fleet was about to shrink even further and cessation of paddle-steamer services would be completed within two decades for Cosens.

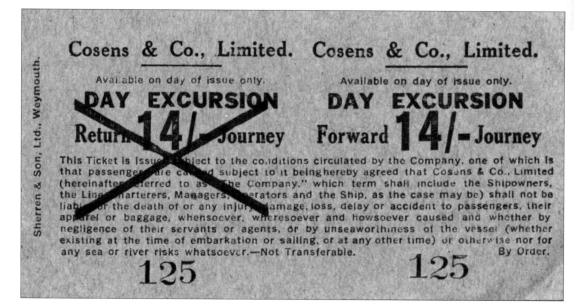

Unlike other operators, Cosens preferred the purser to sell tickets for cruises while walking round the decks. The tickets issued to passengers were very thin and normally fluttered away from passengers in the breeze as they handed over their pennies. Cosens had a simple fare structure and only offered single and day-return tickets. Few single tickets were sold. Pursers of the Cosens fleet were well-known for starting their rounds with pockets full of coins for change. By the time that they returned they were full of pound notes.

Poor weather affected the first post-war season of cruises on some parts of the South Coast. This resulted in around only a quarter of the last full pre-war season of 1938 being carried from Bournemouth Pier. Things were, though, considerably better at Weymouth.

Consul was in a very poor condition after the Second World War but her engine and boiler were in a good condition. At one stage it was suggested that a new hull be built and her engine and boiler installed in it. Ultimately, money was found to refurbish *Consul* for further service for the company.

Emperor of India recommenced her career on 13 July 1948 with an afternoon cruise from Bournemouth to Totland Bay with a full complement of passengers on board. The Emperor of India spent every season serving Bournemouth, apart from 1922, when she was chartered by the Cinque Ports Navigation Company and operated from Brighton. The breaking up of Emperor of India was announced in 1957. She was well-remembered for her cruises from Bournemouth. She was also well-known at Southampton, where she was dry-docked each spring.

On 18 June 1960, *Monarch* operated a special cruise from Bournemouth to Portsmouth to see the arrival of HRH Princess Margaret and her new husband as they returned from their West Indies honeymoon on *Britannia*.

Consul's paddle box while alongside Bournemouth Pier showing the Cosens house flag at the centre.

Albert Victor loading passengers at Weymouth. *Albert Victor* was acquired by Cosens in 1889. She was built in 1883 for service in Scotland. She could act as both a passenger steamer and a tug. By 1928, *Albert Victor* had reached the end of her economic life for Cosens and was withdrawn and scrapped.

Premier at Weymouth harbour around 1905. In June 1932, *Premier* had a bad collision with the submarine *Rainbow*. *Premier*'s bow was damaged but she survived and passengers were transferred to safety at Weymouth. Remarkably, she re-entered service for Cosens around a week later after a very fast repair.

Majestic off St Alban's Head. *Majestic* had her maiden cruise for Cosens on 20 May 1901 when she cruised to the Shambles lightship. She adopted a livery of buff funnel with black top when she entered service. This was better than the black that was used by Cosens' steamers before her introduction. *Majestic* became the flagship of the Cosens fleet.

Emperor of India off Bournemouth Pier. *Emperor of India* made her first trip for Cosens from Weymouth on 24 April 1908. *Emperor of India*'s first-class saloon was richly decorated with fine wood panelling, Utrecht velvet and rich curtains. The steamer was also lit by electric light.

Leaving Bournemouth Pier

Above: Brodick Castle departing from Bournemouth Pier. She had been built by McIntyre & Co. of Paisley in 1878. After service elsewhere, Cosens acquired her in 1901. She had a career of less than ten years with the company.

Right: 1937 provided another opportunity for a fleet review when the Coronation Review of George VI and Queen Elizabeth was held at Spithead on 20 May. *Monarch*, *Emperor of India* and *Victoria* all ran excursions to the review and the spectacular illuminations that followed.

LULWORTH COVE

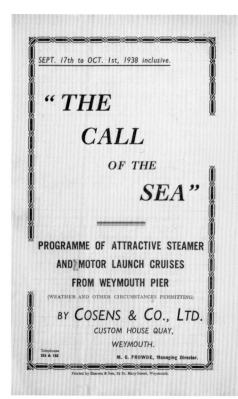

Above: Cosens had an enviable reputation for the upkeep of their paddle steamers. They were also well known for the large amount of deck seating on their steamers. This allowed the maximum number of people to enjoy fine sunny days and the glorious Dorset coastline.

Left: Cosens' 'Call of the Sea' programme of cruises for September and October 1938. The company produced regular timetables throughout each season. For this one in 1938, they operated the regular Lulworth Cove cruise, landing passengers for an hour ashore, as well as cruises to Portland to view the warships.

Above: *Consul* in the attractive harbour at Weymouth. Cosens were synonymous with Weymouth, and the company was one of the major employers as well as one of the biggest sources of income due to the revenue of the paddle steamers, which were so solidly linked with the resort.

Right: Guidebook produced by Cosens around the early 1960s. It gives full details of their services and places visited as well as including numerous photos and advertisements for local businesses.

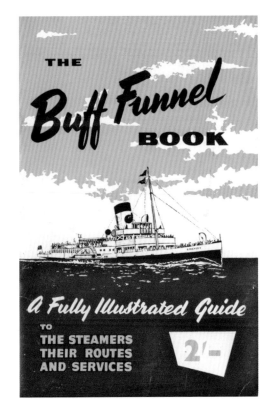

THE

Buff Funnel BOOK

A Fully Illustrated Guide

TO
THE STEAMERS
THEIR ROUTES
AND SERVICES

2/-

Items of crockery used aboard the Cosens steamers during the twentieth century showing the company house flag. The plate was found by divers diving off Totland Bay Pier on the Isle of Wight. Presumably, a galley boy tossed it overboard to avoid doing his chores.

Embassy at Totland Bay Pier. The pier was declared as being unfit for calls by paddle steamers in the early 1930s. Yarmouth then replaced Totland as the calling point for Cosens. It was to be another twenty years before the pier was reopened for paddle-steamer services.

Above: *Consul* cruising off Old Harry Rocks at the end of her career for Cosens. The Dorset coast provided one of the most scenic cruising areas of the UK for paddle-steamer passengers.

Right: Handbill advertising special cruises for 'Navy Days' at Portland Dockyard by Cosens' paddle steamers. Navy Days were hugely popular events and passengers enjoyed a cruise that would enable them to see the Royal Navy fleet in the dockyard and to meet the crew. Cosens ran hourly cruises to Portland and admission fees to the dockyard went to Royal Navy charities.

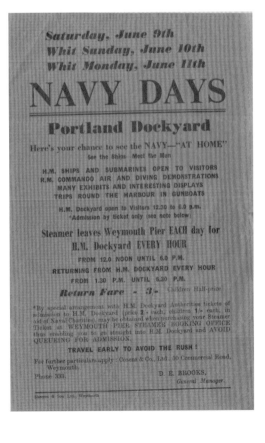

Saturday, June 9th
Whit Sunday, June 10th
Whit Monday, June 11th

NAVY DAYS

Portland Dockyard

Here's your chance to see the NAVY—"AT HOME"
See the Ships Meet the Men

H.M. SHIPS AND SUBMARINES OPEN TO VISITORS
R.M. COMMANDO AIR AND DIVING DEMONSTRATIONS
MANY EXHIBITS AND INTERESTING DISPLAYS
TRIPS ROUND THE HARBOUR IN GUNBOATS

H.M. Dockyard open to Visitors 12.30 to 6.0 p.m.
*Admission by ticket only (see note below)

Steamer leaves Weymouth Pier EACH day for
H.M. Dockyard EVERY HOUR

FROM 12.0 NOON UNTIL 6.0 P.M.
RETURNING FROM H.M. DOCKYARD EVERY HOUR
FROM 1.30 P.M. UNTIL 6.30 P.M.

Return Fare - 3/- Children Half-price

*By special arrangement with H.M. Dockyard Authorities tickets of
admission to H.M. Dockyard (price 2/- each, children 1/- each, in
aid of Naval Charities) may be obtained when purchasing your Steamer
Ticket at WEYMOUTH PIER STEAMER BOOKING OFFICE
thus enabling you to go straight into H.M. Dockyard and AVOID
QUEUEING FOR ADMISSION.

TRAVEL EARLY TO AVOID THE RUSH !

For further particulars apply : Cosens & Co., Ltd., 30 Commercial Road,
Weymouth.
Phone 333.
D. E. BROOKS,
General Manager.

Cosens & Son, Ltd., Weymouth

Consul at Lulworth Cove in 1961. The cove is a scenic gem and a cruise on a Cosens paddle steamer gave passengers the perfect opportunity to relax on the beach and to paddle in the crystal-clear water that can be appreciated in this view. Note the gangway and exit from the bow of the *Consul*. This was almost unique to Cosens.

Consul at Lulworth Cove in 1961. *Consul* made her last Lulworth Cove run in September 1962.

Right: Passengers boarding the *Consul* at Lulworth Cove in 1961. This image shows the gangway that was constructed to enable passengers to disembark from the steamer onto the beach. It may not conform to modern health and safety standards, but it provided an excellent means of reaching the beach from steamers for many decades at Lulworth.

Below: Consul approaching Weymouth towards the end of her career. The 1950s saw more focus on motor coaches as a way of attracting extra business. Coach operators were canvassed to try and attract coach-party bookings to link in with holidays at South Coast resorts such as Weymouth.

Consul at Weymouth in September 1962. Her long and happy career operating along the Dorset cruise for Cosens was almost at an end.

Consul departing from Weymouth Pleasure Pier in July 1955. The mid 1950s seemed to be badly affected by poor weather as well as other national and international threats to trading. This led to the *Emperor of India* being withdrawn at the end of 1956. By this time she was ageing and lacked the flexibility and sailing ability of the other steamers.

Consul tied up at Weymouth on 31 October 1962. *Consul* gained great popularity as the Cosens paddle steamer that landed passengers from the bow along a plank onto the beach at Lulworth Cove.

Above: By 1962, when this photograph was taken of *Consul*, the Cosens fleet had shrunk significantly from its initial post-war height. At the end of that year, *Consul* would be withdrawn and it would then just leave *Embassy* to carry on the Cosens tradition of operating pleasure steamers.

Left: *Embassy* approaching Yarmouth Pier on 28 June 1963. *Embassy* undertook a great number of Isle of Wight sailings at the time. Five shilling non-landing cruises from Totland Bay to Bournemouth were offered and proved to be popular.

Embassy arriving at Bournemouth on 4 July 1966. That year saw her encounter some technical problems as well as issues over inadequate advertising. Such small things could greatly affect the viability of paddle steamers during those declining years. Poor weather followed, and by the end of the season it was apparent that *Embassy* was facing major challenges.

Consul at Weymouth in August 1962. She regularly undertook cruises to the Shambles lightship during the early 1960s. In connection with this, a crew member collected newspapers and other items from passengers. These items were then transferred to the lightship via a heaving line and bucket to supply the men and to entertain the passengers.

Embassy at Poole. Embassy's final day in service was on 22 September 1966. After this, she sailed from Bournemouth to Weymouth for what was thought to be her normal winter lay-up. When she was offered for sale by Cosens in December 1966, she was advertised as being suitable as a floating casino, restaurant or clubhouse.

Embassy at Weymouth prior to her departure to the breakers'. With major work being required to equip *Embassy* for the 1967 season it was decided that she would have to be withdrawn. Cosens issued a statement saying, 'This is a sad day for us, but the day of the paddle steamer is over'. At the same time on the River Thames, the venerable General Steam Navigation Company made a similar statement and withdrew from operating their fleet of pleasure steamers. An era was at an end not just at Weymouth but indeed around the UK. *Embassy* was towed away from Weymouth for the final time on 25 May 1967 to go to the shipbreakers' at Ghent.

Above: *Consul* at Greenwich Pier in September 1963. When *Consul* returned to the Thames in 1963, it was to her birthplace at Blackwall. She hadn't been back to the Thames and London since being launched in 1896. For her time at Sussex and the Thames, her chief engineer was George Taylor.

Right: Handbill for *Consul*'s cruises from Brighton Palace Pier in 1963. *Consul*'s first cruise from Brighton in August 1963 resulted in her carrying just over 100 passengers on the one-hour cruise at a speed of 10 knots. Tony McGinnity praised the success of the *Consul* and stated that a larger paddle steamer capable of 17 knots and capable of carrying 1,400 passengers would run alongside her during the 1964 season.

PALACE PIER, BRIGHTON

CHANNEL SAILINGS

BY

Paddle Steamer **"CONSUL"**

SPECIAL SAILINGS

ON

SUNDAYS TUESDAYS

AND

WEDNESDAYS

Coastal Cruises		Return Fare	
Leave	Back By	Adult	Child
11.30	12.30	5/-	2/6
2.15	3.15	5/-	2/6
Channel Cruise			
3.30	5.30	7/6	2/6
Newhaven Harbour		Single Fare	
5.45		2/6	1/6

Conditions Weather Permitting (Pier Toll NOT Included in Fares)

FULLY LICENSED BAR OPEN ON BOARD

Consul at Weymouth in September 1964. In that year it was announced that *Consul* would once again operate from Weymouth but this time it was for her new owners and not for Cosens. Faced with yet more restrictions and challenges for future operation, *Consul* returned to Weymouth for battle with the *Princess Elizabeth*. The *Princess Elizabeth* had her booking office at the pier entrance and *Consul*, faced with the advertising supremacy of the *Princess Elizabeth*, reacted with a big publicity campaign to attract the dwindling market. It was a sad but admirable sight to see the enthusiasm of operators trying to keep the paddle steamers operating.

Consul returned to Weymouth for the 1964 season and started her cruise programme on 16 May. Her return to Weymouth meant that the already limited market was squeezed even further. *Consul* was lucky in that she was able to land at Lulworth Cove. *Princess Elizabeth* couldn't do that.

STEAMER AT LANDING STAGE

LULWORTH COVE

DURDLE DOOR

MAN OF WAR BAY

CASTLE INN

LULWORTH CASTLE

THE DUCK POND

BAT HEAD   L.6209

Lulworth Cove was a popular destination for Cosens. A cruise from nearby Weymouth was short and gave people the opportunity of a short and affordable cruise along the spectacular coastline. Landing on the beach was an exciting feature for passengers. The many natural features of the coastline and Lulworth can be appreciated on this postcard.

Consul's post-war refit was finally completed at the start of the 1949 season. During the refit she had undergone extensive work on her hull and her saloon was enlarged. In addition, a new enclosed wheelhouse was fitted and a better funnel was installed.

Cosens & Co. were thinking about investing in a new and large steamer to undertake longer and hopefully very lucrative services. The inability to have a steamer built quickly was an issue as shipyards had busy order books to replace wartime losses. With this and the fact that the present fleet was adequate and fit-for-purpose, it meant that they were able to have a post-war that was unlike other major operators, who built new steamers to replace wartime losses. They also hadn't lost any steamers during the war so had less need to build new pleasure steamers.

Consul approaching the Pleasure Pier at Weymouth in post-war years. The hotels lining the promenade at Weymouth provided a fine sight for those arriving by paddle steamer. Cosens were well-known for the punctuality of the steamers in their fleet.

Consul towards the end of her career for Cosens. *Consul* was the last paddle steamer to be slipped at Cosens' yard at Weymouth. *Consul* spent nine weeks on the slipway undergoing her usual winter examination and repairs at Weymouth on 10 May 1961. Several new plates were fitted at the time.

Empress at Weymouth viewed from the Town Bridge. Towards the end of her career, *Empress* was used in the film *Great Expectations*, starring John Mills. Due to her age, *Empress* was well-suited to her film role. Work was carried out to transform her into an early Thames paddle steamer. The filming was done on the River Medway in Kent where Dickens had lived and had based his novel. The most dramatic scene that *Empress* took part in was when the boat of the convict Magwitch was smashed by the heavy paddle wheel.

Empress (*left*) and *Victoria* (*right*) at Weymouth. The initial post-war fleet of four paddle steamers was an excellent one and, when combined with their refits and pattern of cruises, they could have provided a rock-solid service. Other external issues affected their success.

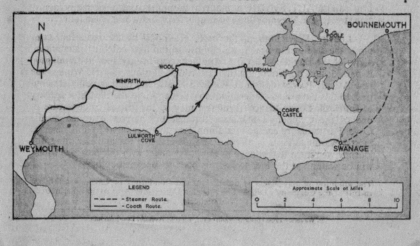

Combined Steamer and Motor Coach Tour of the

Beauty Spots of Dorset

by Messrs. COSENS & COMPANY'S BUFF FUNNEL STEAMERS and
SOUTHERN NATIONAL LUXURY MOTOR COACHES

leaving

BOURNEMOUTH PIER 10.45 am

Due back about 6.0 p.m.

SAILINGS WEATHER AND CIRCUMSTANCES PERMITTING

Up to JUNE 30th — EVERY THURSDAY

From JULY 1st—EVERY TUESDAY, WEDNESDAY & THURSDAY

INCLUSIVE **16/6** FARE

Children under 14 years 9s. 6d.

All steamers have well-fitted Dining Saloons where Light Refreshments
are served; also Fully-Licensed Saloons are open

TICKETS FOR THIS TOUR MUST BE OBTAINED **PRIOR TO DEPARTURE**
FROM THE **STEAMER OFFICE, PIER APPROACH**

Phone Bournemouth 24021

MAP OF THE TOUR

Handbill advertising combined steamer and motor-coach tours of Dorset by Cosens'
paddle steamers. Combined paddle steamer and charabanc services had become
popular during the late 1920s. Many of these gave steamer passengers the opportunity
to sample the many scenic delights of Dorset or the Isle of Wight. Often, these tours
would be combined with lunches or teas at local hotels.

Cosens weren't solely dependent on their paddle steamer fleet. They had other diversified activities which meant that the company wasn't reliant on steamers alone. This included ship repairing and engineering and cold storage. They continued in this role for many years but ship repairs declined later as vessels became larger or were able to use better-located repair facilities.

Embassy entering Poole harbour. 1952 was the last season when Cosens operated a large fleet of six paddle steamers on a wide variety of excursion sailings. Three were based at Bournemouth and lying overnight at Poole, and three sailed from Weymouth.

The engine control platform on the *Embassy* in 1961.

Monarch picking up passengers at Bournemouth Pier. Cosens had a great love of cheap second-hand steamers. They rarely, in over one hundred years, built revolutionary new or large steamers.

Monarch at Bournemouth Pier in July 1959 with a banner mentioning the film *Ferry to Hong Kong*.

In 1961, *Embassy* continued to provide her main programme of cruises until 21 September and then returned to Weymouth for winter lay-up. She had celebrated her Goldn Jubilee a month earlier on 25 August 1961., During that year, Captain Haines was her master along with Alf Plover as Chief Engineer. On 27 August, the Paddle Steamer Preservation society celebrated the Golden Jubilee of *Embassy*. During this, toasts were made, champagne was drunk and a special cake was cut. The cake included a model of the steamer and was cut by Captain Haines.

She had originally been named *Duchess of Norfolk* and was built in 1911 by Henderson & Sons on the Clyde. She mainly operated the ferry service between Portsmouth and Ryde. Her arrival at Weymouth as *Embassy* was praised and she was seen as a particularly good addition to the Cosens fleet. Her first cruise was on 26 July 1937 on a trip from Weymouth to the Isle of Wight.

THE QUAY, POOLE   M 1333

Above: Embassy (front) at Poole. From
2 July to 10 September 1961, *Embassy*
was based at Poole and mainly undertook
Bournemouth cruises. She usually made
two sailings a day between Sundays and
Thursdays to the Isle of Wight and Totland
on all days, apart from Wednesdays to
Yarmouth. On Tuesdays and Thursdays,
the Totland service started from Swanage.
Embassy was employed on the Swanage
ferry service on Fridays. She also undertook
several music cruises.

Left: Embassy's engine in 1961.

Embassy at Bournemouth in 1963. The success of cheap day excursions to the Isle of Wight every Friday from Poole, Swanage and Bournemouth in 1962 was repeated during the 1963 season.

THE PIER, SWANAGE

K 9344

Monarch at Swanage. This view shows the excellent location of Swanage Pier with the cliffs and Old Harry Rocks in the distance. You can also see a very long queue in this image waiting for the steamer to call.

Consul departing from Weymouth during her post-war heyday. During 1960, *Consul*'s visits to Bournemouth were cut. Additional Lulworth Cove cruises replaced them. By this time, Cosens were facing the fact that passengers were losing their love affair with the paddle steamer. It was clear that major changes were occurring. Cosens reacted by changing and juggling services to try and halt the decline. But, with poor weather and other external factors, it was a waste of time and the company was losing a great deal of money. In 1960, Cosens lost £15,000 from their paddle steamer fleet.

    Consul experienced a mixed and ultimately sad end during the 1960s, when attempts to preserve and operate her failed. One of the passengers on *Consul*'s last cruise out of Weymouth was Bob Mills, who was the publican of the Swan Inn at Weymouth. His nostalgic trip reminded him of his time as Chief Engineer on the steamer during the Second World War. He spent this final emotional cruise as Assistant Engineer for the last time. Bob had also been an engineer aboard the *Empress* for Cosens. He also ran the 52-passenger *Topaz* from Weymouth Pier each summer.

Passengers disembarking from the *Consul* at Lulworth Cove.

Consul at Weymouth in September 1957. By this time, the paddle steamer was in decline all around the coastline of the UK.

Paddle Steamer "Embassy"

COSENS & CO., LTD., | **Tel: Bournemouth 24021**

MIDNIGHT CRUISE Every Thursday

WEATHER AND OTHER CIRCUMSTANCES PERMITTING

SOMETHING NEW FOR PARTY OUTINGS
with the unique opportunity of seeing the
Lovely Lights of Swanage and Bournemouth
from the Sea.

(DRESS INFORMAL)

SHOWBOAT

Dancing on Deck

Cabaret

Sing Song in the Saloon

(Fun for the Young and Older)

Depart BOURNEMOUTH PIER 8-30 p.m.
Arrive POOLE Midnight
(Transport Back Arranged)

FARE 11/6 (Special Rates for Parties over 12 persons)

Early Booking at Steamer Office or Pay on Board
Buffet and Fully Licenced Bars Open till Midnight

WAVERLEY PRESS (BOURNEMOUTH) LTD., Lincoln Avenue, Bournemouth

Handbill for showboat cruises by *Embassy*. In 1961, the *Embassy* offered jazz cruises from Bournemouth. One of the jazz bands was the young Kenny Ball, whose appearance attracted 100 more passengers than at the previous month's event. Holidaymakers on the pier watched in fascination when over 450 jean-clad teenagers jived on the deck.

Embassy was returned to Cosens at the end of the Second World War in a terrible condition. Extensive work was carried out to equip her for service in the years after the war. This work included a lot of her wooden decking and steel plating being renewed. A new saloon, bridge and deck house were also added. Her post-war refit was finished off with her being converted to burn oil.

Advertisement for jazz cruises from Bournemouth Pier. The late 1950s saw a surge in interest in jazz music and Cosens were quick to react to this by introducing cruises to appeal to younger passengers. Many famous jazz musicians played aboard the steamers.

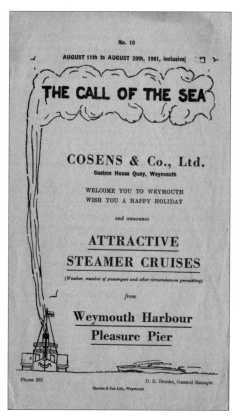

No. 10

AUGUST 11th to AUGUST 20th, 1961, inclusive

THE CALL OF THE SEA

COSENS & Co., Ltd.
Custom House Quay, Weymouth

WELCOME YOU TO WEYMOUTH
WISH YOU A HAPPY HOLIDAY

and announce

ATTRACTIVE
STEAMER CRUISES

(Weather, number of passengers and other circumstances permitting)

from

Weymouth Harbour
Pleasure Pier

Phone 333   D. E. Brooks, General Manager.

Sherren & Son Ltd., Weymouth

Above: Consul in Weymouth Bay on 2
September 1962. *Consul*'s season during 1962
was confined to short cruises from Weymouth
and to Lulworth Cove. Her one long cruise to
Swanage and Bournemouth on 20 June that
year was cancelled due to poor weather. Her
1962 season finished on 20 September.

Left: The familiar buff-coloured programme
listing cruises by Cosens from Weymouth,
dating from 1961. The cruises at the time
included regular trips to Portland to see the
shipping, trips to Lulworth Cove, short coffee
cruises and jazz jamborees. In addition, some
longer trips were offered to Bournemouth,
Swanage and the Isle of Wight.

A deck view aboard the *Consul*. She undertook a cruise to view the first international offshore powerboat race that raced between Cowes and Torquay on 19 August 1961. During that year, *Consul* was based principally at Weymouth. She undertook cruises to Swanage and Bournemouth on Tuesdays and Thursdays between 4 July and 14 September and had an additional double run from Bournemouth to Swanage to place her in direct competition with the *Swanage Queen*. *Consul* departed a quarter of an hour before *Swanage Queen*, so was able to take a lot of the trade.

Embassy alongside Bournemouth Pier in 1960. Cosens were still providing an extensive and attractive timetable in 1960 despite the fact that the paddle steamer was in decline. The timetable was an excellent attempt to mix short and longer cruises along with music and entertainment cruises. Poor weather during the summer further damaged what was already a precarious state of affairs. Cosens inevitably had to react to losses by withdrawing the *Monarch* and placing the *Embassy* on the Bournemouth station. It was clear that Cosens were facing more than enough challenges and future operations would be even leaner.

Captain Harry Defrates was the popular master of the *Consul* in 1952 before moving to the *Monarch*. He returned as *Consul*'s master in 1957–9 before returning to the *Monarch* in 1960.

View of the *Consul*'s bow on 29 July 1962 at Weymouth. In 1964, Captain Holleyoak of the *Consul* was prosecuted for carrying 246 passengers when he could only carry 230. He was fined £10 for a breach of marine regulations. At one time, the *Consul* could carry over 400 passengers but her certificate at the time limited her to 230. Captain Holleyoak was saddened by the event and announced his intention to retire as master after the fine was announced. (J&C McCutcheon Collection)

A steamer at Totland Bay Pier on the Isle of Wight.

Totland Bay Pier was a popular addition to Isle of Wight calling points from 1951 onwards. Despite being in poor condition for many years, it was rebuilt for steamer services. Cosens then commenced operating from Bournemouth to Totland Bay on a regular basis.

Embassy at Bournemouth in the 1960s.

DORSET COUNTY FEDERATION OF YOUNG FARMERS' CLUBS

21st Anniversary Cruise

Licensed Bars, Buffet, Dancing on Board

Thursday, 29th July 1965

8.30 p.m. — Midnight

Admission 10/- (by ticket only)
rights of admission reserved

N⁰ 488

Report to P.S. Embassy in Poole Quay not later than 8.30 p.m.

Subject to conditions of carriage as displayed in Messrs. Cosens & Co. Ltd. Office

Ticket for a charter cruise in July 1965 aboard the *Embassy* from Poole. By 1965, the position for Cosens at Weymouth was looking bleak and, despite enthusiasts hoping that the company would survive as operators of paddle steamers for many more decades, the end was fast approaching.

Consul in Weymouth Bay. Cosens made a net trading loss of £3,794 for 1961. It was stated that the steamers had made a larger profit than in 1960 due to the reduced number of cruises from Bournemouth. The financial report showed that *Monarch* had raised a figure of £2,462.

The well-loved Cosens calling point of Lulworth Cove provided a popular calling point for over a century. Today, regular calls are still made to Lulworth by the pleasure steamers *Balmoral* and *Waverley*.

ALL ABOARD!   DON'T MISS!

★ THE SPECIAL ★ EVENING CRUISE

BY P.S. "CONSUL"

TOWARDS LULWORTH COVE

*   *   *

FROM WEYMOUTH PIER
WEDNESDAY, AUG., 16TH 1961

at 7.30 p.m.   (two hour cruise)

**Viewing Osmington, Ringstead
and Durdle Dor, etc.**

*   *   *

Competitions, Fun & Games For All

FARE 7/- HALF PRICE CHILDREN

TICKETS AVAILABLE ON BOARD

A 'PADDLE STEAMER PRESERVATION SOCIETY' CHARTER

WHICH NO ONE SHOULD MISS

W. J. ADAMS (Bournemouth), LTD.

The Paddle Steamer Preservation Society did a great deal to promote and save paddle steamers from 1959 onwards. It organised many charters of well-loved paddle steamers such as the *Consul* to support Cosens. This handbill advertised a cruise from Weymouth Pleasure Pier in August 1961.

The Paddle Steamer Preservation Society charter of *Embassy* on 5 July 1964 was the first round-the-Isle of Wight cruise from Bournemouth since 1958. It was also the first on a Sunday since 1949.

An early view showing *Embassy* with her original paddle box emblem. Bunting and flags are being hoisted for a special event. When *Embassy* entered service for the Cosens fleet in 1937, she retained her original carved paddle box crest from her railway steamer days. This wasn't changed until after the Second World War when she underwent a refit to equip her for further service after the conflict.

A view of Bournemouth's famous pier. Bournemouth opened a new pier in 1861. Cosens' steamer *Prince* was one of the first callers at the newly opened pier and brought around 100 passengers from Weymouth to witness the gaiety in the town. The new pier was around 1,000 feet long and had much-improved landing facilities for paddle steamers. Just a few years later, around a third of the pier structure was destroyed during storms. By 1880, Bournemouth Pier had been rebuilt to a design by the eminent pier designer Eugenius Birch at a cost of £21,600. Pier-head buildings were added in 1885.

Emperor of India berthed in Weymouth harbour, with *Premier* and another of the fleet to her right. (J&C McCutcheon Collection)

Above: Monarch arriving at Bournemouth Pier on 28 July 1957. (J&C McCutcheon Collection)

Left: Monarch's Lounge Bar towards the end of her career. It shows the rather old-fashioned look that was unlike newer pleasure steamers such as *Royal Sovereign* or *Balmoral*.

In 1952, *Monarch* was in her second season with Cosens. By this time, the Cosens house flag had replaced the 'SR' on the paddle boxes. Most significantly, the first-class refreshment saloon (lower deck aft) had been transformed into a fine dining saloon. It served afternoon teas, cold meals and other light refreshments. It was, though, hard to disguise the fact that *Monarch* was once a Southern Railway steamer and the basic passenger accommodation towards the bow made her familiar as a former two-class paddle steamer.

Monarch's paddle box. The paddle box was normally decorated in some way with vents and a central carved wooden emblem. *Monarch*'s paddle box shows the Cosens house flag at the centre.

Monarch at Bournemouth Pier. In 1952, if you were lucky enough, you could see up to four of the six Cosens paddle steamers in a day at places such as Bournemouth. On 14 August for example, the *Emperor of India* visited while on longer excursion sailings, *Consul* and *Monarch* served the Swanage service and *Victoria* served Bournemouth from Weymouth.

Monarch off Swanage on 5 July 1958. A year later, *Monarch* was set adrift from her summer berth at Poole on 28 June 1959. After drifting in the Channel, she was secured by the tug *Wendy Ann* and taken back to her moorings. During the incident, the *Bournemouth Belle* was hit by the bow of the *Monarch* but no damage was inflicted on either vessel.

Monarch towards the end of her life. Cosens reacted to the late 1950s decline by introducing entertainment cruises. These were intended to appeal to the younger generations who were no longer prepared to sit in a deckchair. Twist and jazz bands were engaged to entertain the youngsters. Cabaret artists were also engaged for these special cruises.

Monarch at Bournemouth Pier. Her final cruise for the company was on 8 September 1960. With the withdrawal of the *Monarch* from the South Coast, there was an opening for others to try and squeeze more business out of the dwindling trade. While this was an admirable thing to do, it was ultimately destined to fail.

Monarch on 10 August 1959. Cosens were similar to most other operators in the UK during the mid-1950s when they decided to withdraw some of their largest and most famous paddle steamers. All operators were facing the same challenges and most faced this by withdrawing old and large steamers and keeping newer ones in service.

Monarch arriving at Bournemouth Pier during her final years of service. *Monarch* was the final paddle steamer purchased by Cosens. Originally built as *Shanklin* for the Southern Railway, she initially operated the Portsmouth–Ryde ferry service for the railway company.

Monarch was sold in January 1961 to breakers at Cork. An attempt was made to tow her from Weymouth on 31 January but had to be abandoned due to poor weather. Eventually she departed from Weymouth on 1 March, towed by the tug *Salvonia*. *Monarch* was sold due to economy and because she was still a coal burner.

A fine view showing a Cosens paddle steamer reversing out of Lulworth Cove. The steep cliffs down to the pleasant beach can be appreciated fully in this view.

Consul viewed from the beach during one of her regular calls. These calls ceased when Cosens closed services in the mid-1960s. In recent years, the famous pleasure steamer *Balmoral* visited the cove to land passengers but this was done by motor boat and not by the traditional wooden gangway.

Consul alongside Weymouth Pleasure Pier in September 1962. Note the familiar large yellow posters advertising sailings on the deck house as well as a blackboard giving details of the cruise on offer to people promenading on the pier. You can also see the canvas dodgers along the top of the bridge wings to provide some extra protection for the bridge crew.

Above: Consul at Bournemouth Pier in 1961. *Monarch* and *Consul* had many cruises cancelled due to poor weather in 1961. *Consul* didn't have an off-service day that season but started her weekend services after lunchtime. *Embassy* had her off-service day on Saturday.

Left: A view aboard *Consul* around 1960. *Consul* was very much a Victorian paddle steamer and possessed great charm.

Opposite above: Consul's engine room. A paddle steamer's engine was always a great attraction for enthusiasts as well as those who wanted some warmth on a cold blustery day. Being able to see the engine moving was a central attraction to a paddle steamer.

Consul cruising off Swanage on 5 July 1958. The mid-1950s seemed to be badly affected by poor weather as well as other national and international threats to trading.

EVENING ECHO, BOURNEMOUTH, Saturday, May 29   Page 5

BUFF FUNNEL STEAMERS

COSENS & CO. LTD. Tel. Bournemouth 24021

SEASON STARTS SATURDAY, JUNE 5th

WITH A SAIL ROUND THE ISLE OF WIGHT BY SEA. Depart Swanage 10 a.m., fare 26s. Depart Bournemouth 11 a.m., fare 23s. 6d. (3s. 6d. off if booked before day of sailing. Children half). Back at Bournemouth 7 p.m., Swanage 7.45 p.m., Poole 8.45 p.m.

SWANAGE SERVICE Sundays and Tuesdays (other days by motor vessel). Depart Bournemouth 10.45 a.m. and 2.30 p.m. Fare 10s. return, 5/- single.

ISLE OF WIGHT SAILINGS at 10.30 a.m. and 2.30 p.m. on **Mondays,** fare 15s.; **Wednesdays and Thursdays,** fare 19s. return.

ISLE OF WIGHT TOUR Wednesdays and Thursdays, fare 28s.

For full details of **AFTERNOON TRIPS** and fares apply Steamer Office or Information Bureau for leaflet.

EVENING CRUISES every Sunday. Depart 7.45 p.m. Fare 6s. 6d.

Advanced booking advised.   Bar and Buffet always open

Newspaper advertisement for Cosens' services from Bournemouth. It was cheaper to book a cruise in advance. It cost £1.30 for the cruise round the Isle of Wight from Swanage.

Embassy with *Swanage Queen* behind her at Poole in 1961. The Paddle Steamer Preservation Society had been formed in 1959 and had been inspired by the withdrawal of the *Freshwater* at Lymington. She later appeared as *Sussex Queen* and for 1961, her name was changed again to *Swanage Queen*. Her owner, Herbert Jennings, wanted to place her in service along the Sussex Coast from Swanage. She entered service in July 1961. She was, of course, competition to Cosens at a time when they could do without it.

Embassy in Southampton Water on 6 July 1966. It was a season that was beset by all of the usual challenges of the mid-1960s for Cosens and other operators. Matters were made worse by events such as the seamen's strike, which meant that services by Cosens were affected. The usual excuse of poor weather was also blamed along with small boat tragedies.

Embassy alongside at Weymouth on 28 April 1966. The 1966 season had been mixed for *Embassy*. Advertising was criticised and external events affected trade. The company were examining the future of the *Embassy* and whether she had a long-term future, especially due to her age. Paddle steamers required a great deal of maintenance and investment to keep them in good working order and it was apparent that *Embassy* would only remain in service for a short time longer.

When all the paddle steamers had been withdrawn, Sidney Davis of Cosens said, 'We carried millions of passengers and never lost one of them'. (J&C McCutcheon Collection)

Embassy's lounge looking astern.

Left: Embassy on 6 July 1966. With the fitting of a new mainmast in 1966, *Embassy* was fitted with electric-powered navigation lights rather than the old oil-powered ones. The national seamen's strike in 1966 greatly affected Cosens as well as other operators around the UK like the General Steam Navigation Company.

Below: Advertisement for cruises by the *Embassy* from Bournemouth Pier to the Isle of Wight in 1966. When *Embassy* was withdrawn, Bournemouth Council endeavored to find another operator to place another steamer in service from the pier. The *St Trillo* of North Wales was the popular candidate to replace *Embassy* at Bournemouth.

Paddle Steamer 'EMBASSY'
(COSENS & CO., LTD.)

Monday, 1st Aug. & Wednesday, 3rd Aug.

SPECIAL CRUISE through the SOLENT to COWES ROADS, anchoring to view the ROYAL REGATTA

SAILS FROM BOURNEMOUTH PIER
MONDAY, 1st AUGUST: Sails 10.30 a.m.; back by 5.30 p.m.
WEDNESDAY, 3rd AUGUST: Sails 10.30 a.m.; back by 6.45 p.m.

FARE: 30/-; CHILDREN: HALF PRICE

Lunch and licensed snack bar available on board
Book now at Steamer Office, Pier Approach (Tel.: B'mouth 24021)

Above: Embassy in Weymouth Bay.

Right: Embassy's Tea Room in the early 1960s.
The old-style furniture and vases of flowers give the
saloon a homely touch.

Above: Embassy on 6 July 1966. *Embassy* made her final sailing for Cosens on 22 September 1966. This cruise effectively ended the Cosens tradition that had started a century earlier.

Left: Embassy tied up at Weymouth.

Embassy at sea during the 1950s. The early 1950s was a challenging period for Cosens and the company was armed with a myriad of excuses to blame losses on. Poor weather inevitably ranked as a prime excuse but the increasing usage of cars and motor coaches caused damage. Things deepened even further in the following decade.

Embassy at Weymouth. *Embassy* had a compound steam engine, which allowed her to cruise at a speed of 13.5 knots. Both *Embassy* and *Monarch* were fitted with bow rudders. (J&C McCutcheon Collection)

Cosens & Company Ltd.
PS 'Embassy'

Sailings between Bournemouth and the Isle of Wight for 1962

Period June 3rd to July 14th
EVERY MONDAY, WEDNESDAY AND THURSDAY

Period July 15th to September 8th
EVERY DAY EXCEPT FRIDAY AND SATURDAY

	Dep. B'th.	Dep. I.o.W.	Arr. B'th.
Combined Steamer and Motor Coach Tour of the Isle of Wight (Fare 24/6)	10.0 a.m.	4.45 p.m.	6.30 p.m.
Full Day Trip to the Isle of Wight (4½ hours ashore.) (Fare 16/-)	10.0 a.m.	4.45 p.m.	6.30 p.m.
Morning Cruise to the Isle of Wight (not landing). (Fare 10/6)	10.0 a.m.	11.30 a.m.	1.00 p.m.
*Afternoon Cruise to the Isle of Wight (about 1 hour ashore) (Fare 12/6)	2.30 p.m.	4.45 p.m.	6.30 p.m.
*Isle of Wight Single Trip only, Fare 10/-	10.0 a.m.	2.30 p.m.	

*Not on Thursdays after June 17th from that date Thursdays dept. time will be 3.30 p.m. (not 2.30 p.m.) Not Landing. Fare 10/6.
Landing at Yarmouth Wednesdays. Other days Totland

EVERY FRIDAY (From 22nd June 1962)
CHEAP DAY EXCURSION. FARE 12/6

Dept. Poole 8.30 a.m.; Swanage 9.30 a.m.; Bournemouth 10.30 a.m.
Arrive Yarmouth 12 noon. Depart Yarmouth 3.30 p.m.
Arrive Bournemouth 5.0 p.m.; Swanage 6.0 p.m.; Poole passengers may have to land at Bournemouth
Coach trip to RYDE 5/6 extra, if asked for on boarding Steamer

OR

A Cruise through the Solent to Cowes landing for about 1¼ hours.
Arrive Cowes 1.15 p.m. Depart Cowes 2.30 p.m. other return times as above. FARE 20/-

Tickets available on board the Steamer for all trips except the Inclusive Coach Tour of I.O.W. which must be obtained at the Steamer Office before sailing. Children under 14 years half fare.

Above: *Embassy* during the 1960s. In 1960, Cosens started their services from Bournemouth on 31 May and their Weymouth services started at Whitsun. Their second Bournemouth steamer was scheduled to appear in late June or early July.

Left: Handbill advertising cruises between Bournemouth and the Isle of Wight during the 1962 season by the *Embassy*. Cosens arranged coach tours of the Isle of Wight to coincide with their paddle steamers.

At the end of paddle-steamer services, when *Embassy* was withdrawn, a Cosens spokesman said, 'This is a sad day for us but the day of the paddle steamer is over'.

Embassy departing from a pier. In this view you can appreciate the extensive open deck that was popular in warm sunny weather. Poor weather was partly blamed for the decline of the Cosens fleet but, in reality, the decline was caused by a number of factors that affected pleasure steamers nationally.

Embassy laid up during the winter adjacent to the Cosens depot at Weymouth on 8 February 1960. From 1960, *Monarch* and *Embassy* underwent bottom scraping and other hull work at the Admiralty slip at Portland.

Embassy on 6 July 1966. Cosens continued operating as a company for several decades after the paddle steamers disappeared. During this time they chiefly undertook engineering work. This was, though, difficult at a time when companies had different requirements to those of the post-war years. Some shipbuilding was also undertaken. Challenges over the position of facilities at Portland, as well as competition elsewhere, meant that by the early 1990s the company was in trouble and Cosens finally ceased to trade in 1996 – 120 years after the great tradition had started.

By the early–mid-1960s, *Embassy* was soldiering on. By this time, the season was opening later than it had in previous decades and *Embassy* undertook her first cruise at the end of May. That old excuse of 'poor weather' didn't affect her during 1964 and she was blessed with excellent weather and queues of passengers.

A view from *Embassy*'s sponson in 1965. *Embassy* had a good season for Cosens in 1965 and was helped by good weather although by the end of the season the weather had deteriorated.

Embassy at Weymouth on 31 October 1962. In 1962, *Embassy* was off service on Fridays and Saturdays at the start of the season. From the end of June, she operated on Fridays from Dorset to Yarmouth at a special cheap fare.

PADDLE STEAMER
'Embassy'
(COSENS & CO., LTD.)

CRUISES TO THE ISLE OF WIGHT

Sailings from Bournemouth Pier on Mondays to Fridays inclusive, allowing time to make motor coach tour of Isle of Wight.

———————

Sailings to Swanage and Poole daily in conjunction with Croson's Motor Vessels

———————

Evening Cruises, etc.

———————

For further details apply to STEAMER OFFICE, PIER APPROACH
Telephone: BOURNEMOUTH 24021

Advertisement for cruises by *Embassy* to the Isle of Wight around the mid 1960s.

COSENS & COMPANY Ltd
PS "EMBASSY"

(For regular daily sailings to Isle of Wight and Swanage, see
Steamer programme)

EVERY FRIDAY

(From 22nd June 1962)

Cheap Day Excursion
TO
Isle of Wight

Landing at Yarmouth
(Approximately 3¼ hours ashore)

Dept. Poole 8.30 a.m.; Swanage 9.30 a.m.; Bournemouth 10.30 a.m.
Arrive Yarmouth 12 noon. Depart Yarmouth 3.30 p.m.
Arrive Bournemouth 5.0 p.m.; Swanage 6.0 p.m.; Poole 7.0 p.m.

Fare 12/6

M/C trip to RYDE for 5/6d. extra, if asked for on boarding the
Steamer

OR

A Cruise through the Solent to Cowes landing for about 1¼ hours.
Arrive Cowes 1.15 p.m. Depart Cowes 2.30 p.m. other return times
as above.

Fare 20/-

Children under 14 years half fare.
Tickets obtainable on board or at Steamer Office, Pier Approach,
Bournemouth

The Proprietors will not be responsible for any accidents, injury or loss of life, or loss of
damage to property of the passengers of whatever nature, while on the Proprietors Vessels,
piers, gangways, or other property of the Poprietors. All advertised sailings are subject to
weather and other circumstances permitting. Proprietors reserve the right to vary times and
cancel sailings without notice. Every endeavour will be made to maintain the advertised
time tables, but no responsibility can be accepted for any loss or delay.

WAVERLEY PRESS (BOURNEMOUTH) LTD., Lincoln Avenue, Bournemouth

Handbill advertising *Embassy*'s Friday sailings to Yarmouth. The 1950s saw several Isle
of Wight piers being used again by the Cosens fleet. Ryde, Ventnor, Cowes and Sandown
all became available once again during the period.

Above: A teapot used aboard Cosens' paddle steamers during post-war years.

Left: Embassy approaching Bournemouth Pier. Post-war years saw the introduction of 'showboat' cruises from Bournemouth. These gained in popularity and soon became an established feature of sailings.

Midships view of *Embassy* at Bournemouth in 1963. Cosens always undertook a great deal of repair work on other pleasure steamers as they had good facilities, a slipway and expertise in their workforce. Even up to 1963, Weymouth was undertaking a great deal of repair work, and large and imposing steamers such as *Bristol Queen* and *Sandown* visited the Cosens yard. This part of Cosens' operation was threatened as the size of the slipway was too small for many steamers and also required repairs. It was therefore soon placed for sale.

COME ABOARD ! !

YOUR FIRST OPPORTUNITY FOR SIX YEARS TO SAIL

ROUND THE ISLE OF WIGHT

(Time ashore at Shanklin)

By Paddle Steamer "EMBASSY"

SUNDAY, 5th JULY, 1964

DEPART BOURNEMOUTH PIER — 2.15 p.m.

DUE BACK ABOUT 9.20 p.m.

FARE - 23/6

N.B.—Tickets May be purchased at a
SPECIAL REDUCED FARE OF 18/- Prior to the day of sailing
Children under 15 half fare
(Fares refunded in the event of cancellation)

THIS IS A MAGNIFICENT 85-MILE CRUISE OF PICTURESQUE SCENERY
PASSING THROUGH THE SMOOTH WATERS OF THE SOLENT AND SPITHEAD,
ROUND THE FORELAND SOUTHWARDS TO SHANKLIN WHERE TIME WILL
BE ALLOWED ASHORE. "EMBASSY" WILL RETURN WESTWARDS PAST
ST. CATHERINE'S POINT AND THE NEEDLES

TEAS and LIGHT REFRESHMENTS AVAILABLE ON BOARD
LICENSED BAR OPEN THROUGHOUT THE SAILING

TICKETS AVAILABLE FROM :

G. V. W. Gray, 22 Gerald Road, Bournemouth
D. L. Dougan, The Mill House, Donyatt, Illminster, Somerset
The Customers' Bureau, Beales, Old Christchurch Road, Bournemouth
or from The Steamer Office, Bottom of West Cliff, Bournemouth

*Promoted by the Paddle Steamer Preservation Society, with the co-operation of
Cosens & Co., Ltd., under whose Conditions of Carriage as exhibited at
their Offices, Agencies and on board their ships passengers are
carried. Sailing subject to weather and circumstances.*

Sherrens - Weymouth

Above: Embassy had a larger funnel fitted when she was converted to burning oil in 1946.

The early 1960s might have been a period of greater stability for Cosens when their fleet was made leaner. It was, though, affected by a period of competition from steamers such as the *Swanage Queen* and *Princess Elizabeth*.

Left: A highlight of the 1964 season for Cosens was the Paddle Steamer Preservation Society charter of the *Embassy* round the Isle of Wight on 5 July. Over 500 enthusiasts and passengers joined *Embassy* for the cruise and it showed that there was still a degree of hope and enthusiasm for the old paddle steamers.

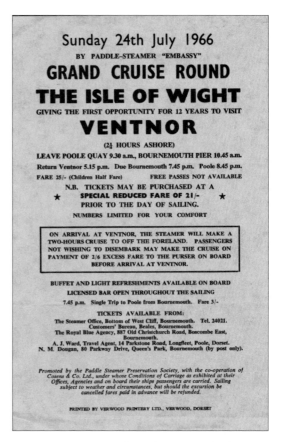

Sunday 24th July 1966
BY PADDLE-STEAMER "EMBASSY"
GRAND CRUISE ROUND
THE ISLE OF WIGHT
GIVING THE FIRST OPPORTUNITY FOR 12 YEARS TO VISIT
VENTNOR
(2½ HOURS ASHORE)

LEAVE POOLE QUAY 9.30 a.m., BOURNEMOUTH PIER 10.45 a.m.
Return Ventnor 5.15 p.m. Due Bournemouth 7.45 p.m. Poole 8.45 p.m.
FARE 25/- (Children Half Fare)   FREE PASSES NOT AVAILABLE
N.B. TICKETS MAY BE PURCHASED AT A
★   SPECIAL REDUCED FARE OF 21/-   ★
PRIOR TO THE DAY OF SAILING.
NUMBERS LIMITED FOR YOUR COMFORT

ON ARRIVAL AT VENTNOR, THE STEAMER WILL MAKE A
TWO-HOURS CRUISE TO OFF THE FORELAND. PASSENGERS
NOT WISHING TO DISEMBARK MAY MAKE THE CRUISE ON
PAYMENT OF 2/6 EXCESS FARE TO THE PURSER ON BOARD
BEFORE ARRIVAL AT VENTNOR.

BUFFET AND LIGHT REFRESHMENTS AVAILABLE ON BOARD
LICENSED BAR OPEN THROUGHOUT THE SAILING
7.45 p.m. Single Trip to Poole from Bournemouth. Fare 3/-

TICKETS AVAILABLE FROM:
The Steamer Office, Bottom of West Cliff, Bournemouth. Tel. 24021.
Customers' Bureau, Beales, Bournemouth.
The Royal Blue Agency, 887 Old Christchurch Road, Boscombe East,
Bournemouth.
A. J. Ward, Travel Agent, 14 Parkstone Road, Longfleet, Poole, Dorset.
N. M. Dougan, 80 Parkway Drive, Queen's Park, Bournemouth (by post only).

Promoted by the Paddle Steamer Preservation Society, with the co-operation of
Cosens & Co. Ltd., under whose Conditions of Carriage as exhibited at their
Offices, Agencies and on board their ships passengers are carried. Sailing
subject to weather and circumstances, but should the excursion be
cancelled fares paid in advance will be refunded.

PRINTED BY VERWOOD PRINTERY LTD., VERWOOD, DORSET

Right: Handbill for a Paddle Steamer
Preservation Society-promoted cruise on
the *Embassy* on in July 1966. The society
worked closely with Cosens to encourage
passengers to join such cruises to try and
keep the paddle steamer tradition alive.

Below: Embassy at Bournemouth Pier
in 1963. Cosens operated many music
cruises in 1962–3. Late night 'Twist and
Jive' cruises were offered as well as jazz
cruises and Poole party nights.

Embassy alongside Bournemouth Pier on Sunday 18 September 1966. This was the last Sunday before her withdrawal. Cosens announced the cessation of paddle steamers and the withdrawal of their last paddle steamer in December 1966. A company spokesman said, 'The last nail in the coffin was that holidaymakers no longer seemed to want to go anywhere over a long time and the emphasis was now on speed'.

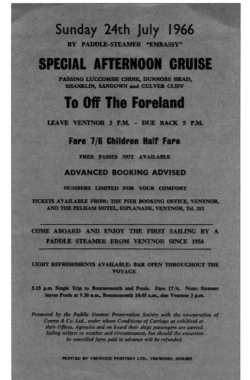

Handbill advertising a special afternoon cruise on the *Embassy* from Ventnor on 24 July 1966. It was the first cruise by a paddle steamer from Ventnor since 1954 and was promoted by the Paddle Steamer Preservation Society. Novelty cruises for enthusiasts were a vital aspect in trying to keep interest and services going.

THERE'S A FIGHT TO KEEP BRITAIN'S OLDEST PADDLE STEAMER GOING

The Consul — in this picture she was being prepared for a summer season. Will she have another?

THE Paddle Steamer Preservation Society are to fight — and fight hard they declare — the withdrawal of Weymouth's sole remaining pleasure steamer, the 277-ton Consul. She is Britain's oldest paddle steamer.

Her owners, Cosens and Company, say she has been losing money for two years. The ship is laid up awaiting a decision on her future, having made her last trip in September.

The society, which recently acted to preserve Britain's smallest paddle steamer, the 76-ton Alum Chine, want a new lease of life for Consul. They would like to see the formation of a small, vigorous committee in Weymouth to obtain the ship.

One of the oldest passenger ships on the British Register, the Consul was built on the Thames in 1896 and for many years operated summer cruises from Weymouth to Lulworth Cove, and along the Dorset coast. Her withdrawal, say the society, will be a blow not only to the people of Weymouth, but also to holiday-

Originally the Duke of Devonshire, the ship was for many years owned by the Devon Dock, Pier and Steamship Company, of Exmouth. In the early-thirties she was sold and spent some time in the South of Ireland, and later the Bristol Channel. She was acquired by her present owners in 1938. In both World Wars she was requisitioned and was on active service as a minesweeper.

Well maintained, and in good condition, she is economical to operate. Unlike many newer steamers that still rely on coal, Consul is oil-fired.

In recent years she has become a celebrated ship, has been featured on Christmas cards and calendars, and figured prominently in the film "The Feathered Wheel" made in 1956.

The withdrawal of the *Consul* resulted in the Paddle Steamer Preservation Society calling a meeting at Weymouth to voice its concerns and to try and get local businesses and people behind a scheme to save the *Consul*. Somewhat surprisingly, Commander Rhodes announced that he planned to operate the *Princess Elizabeth* from Weymouth in 1963. This wasn't what was expected but it did offer the prospect of paddle steamers operating from Weymouth again, ensuring that the Cosens tradition continued. Just a few years later, newspapers would announce the departure of *Embassy* – the last paddle steamer of the Cosens fleet.

Left: Embassy at Weymouth prior to her departure to the breakers' viewed from the stern of the *Princess Elizabeth*. Cosens announced shortly before Christmas that it was to cease its steamer operations and that its last paddle steamer – *Embassy* – was to be sold.

Below: Consul at Weymouth in 1962–3 when she was awaiting her sale. By the end of the 1962 season it was clear that Cosens had had a far from successful year of sailings. The elderly *Consul* was highlighted as being a major loss maker and with impending surveys and no sign of passenger trade or weather improving, Cosens reluctantly withdrew her from service. The once large and proud Cosens fleet had now been shrunk to just one.

Above: *Consul*'s paddle wheel and sponson area during her refit at the Dorset Lakes Shipyard in 1963. This photograph gives a rare opportunity to view her feathering paddle floats.

Right: *Consul* during her refit at the Dorset Lakes Shipyard in 1963.

Consul at Hamworthy Quay at Poole prior to service at Brighton in 1963. The Victorian *Consul* inevitably looked like ending her days at the scrapyard due to her age and condition. But, she was saved and placed in service along the Sussex Coast in 1963. It was hardly a sensible idea due to the underlying problems, but enthusiasm and emotion took over. Straight away, she was beset by a number of structural challenges and, most importantly, her passenger certificate was reduced to 230 from 450 making her ultimately uneconomic.

Consul at Poole prior to service at Brighton. 1963 wasn't a good season for *Consul*, unlike *Embassy* and *Princess Elizabeth*. Her age, condition and lack of versatility stopped her having a lucrative and successful future. Her Sussex sailings were marred by problems. She did, though, manage a week of quite successful cruising with Don Rose's New Belle Steamers on the Thames when she visited some of the well-known routes of the General Steam Navigation Company. 1963 was a disaster for *Consul* away from the Cosens fleet and many thought that it would have been better to see her broken up rather than face an undignified and long-drawn-out end.

Consul viewed from Gravesend with Tilbury docks in the distance in September 1963. *Consul* carried over 1,500 passengers on her trips from London in September 1963. When she operated from Gravesend she departed from the Stuart Road Pier.

Consul approaching Tower Pier, London, in September 1963. She undertook her short season from London when Bermondsey businessman Don Rose's plan to charter the *Medway Queen* to take his customers on a cruise failed due to withdrawal of the *Medway Queen*. *Consul* took her place on the charter cruise on the Sunday.

Consul at Southampton, prior to her service at Weymouth in 1964. The season witnessed challenges and a flurry of paddle-steamer services. In the end, it wasn't possible to provide a profitable service and *Consul*, while performing well and undertaking a sensible pattern of cruises, finally had to be withdrawn and the steamer made her farewell final call at Lulworth on 28 August 1964.

Consul approaching Newhaven on 18 August 1963 during her brief career working in Sussex, Kent and London.

Right: Consul at Weymouth Pleasure Pier on the first day of the season in 1964. The battle between *Consul* and the *Princess Elizabeth* at Weymouth in 1964 would inevitably lead to failure at a time when the paddle steamer faced extinction, as there was a limit to the number of people that wanted a paddle-steamer cruise.

Below: Consul was acquired for use as a static accommodation ship at Dartmouth and she finally left a tearful Weymouth on 4 February 1965. *Consul* was then renamed *Duke of Devonshire*. On her farewell from Weymouth, several key members of her original 1938 crew accompanied her on her departure from her Weymouth base. An era was at an end.

Balmoral at Shanklin. The withdrawal of *Embassy* was a great shock as she had had a new mainmast fitted that year and her saloon had been refurbished. Despite being elderly by the mid-1960s, it was assumed that *Balmoral* would replace her on service from Bournemouth if *Embassy* was withdrawn.

Princess Elizabeth, *Embassy* and *Balmoral* (left to right) at Weymouth in May 1967. Cosens continued ship repairs after their paddle-steamer fleet had disappeared. One of the ships to undergo a refit at Weymouth was the *Balmoral* towards the end of her career with the parent company of Red Funnel.

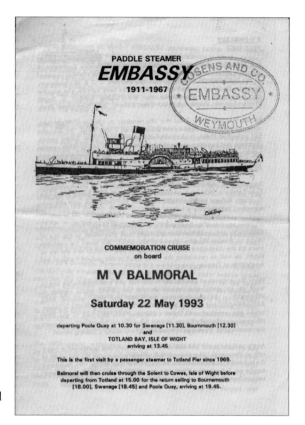

Right: On 22 May 1993, the *Balmoral* undertook a cruise to commemorate the last Cosens paddle steamer – the *Embassy*. During the cruise, *Balmoral* cruised into Lulworth Cove and became the first steamer for many years to do this. She once again took up *Embassy*'s popular route from Poole to Swanage and Bournemouth and gave passengers the opportunity to make the first call by pleasure steamer at Totland Bay Pier since 1969.

Below: The paddle steamer *Waverley* at Torquay in 1979. *Waverley* is now the last seagoing paddle steamer in the world. She keeps the pleasure-steamer tradition alive on her annual visits to the old calling points of Cosens in Dorset, Hampshire and the Isle of Wight.

Balmoral is now the sole survivor of the 1950s' and 1960s' South Coast pleasure-steamer fleet. She provides an important link back to the days of *Consul*, *Monarch* and *Embassy* when she often passed them on her cruises for Red Funnel. She, along with the paddle steamer *Waverley*, keeps the routes of Cosens alive. *Balmoral* now provides the best vantage point to enjoy the spectacular Dorset Coast. www.mvbalmoral.org.uk

Kingswear Castle was built in 1924 for service on the River Dart. After four decades of service there, she was withdrawn and later restored on the River Medway. In 2012 she returned to the River Dart. She now provides cruises on the Dart, where Cosens once operated. The great tradition of pleasure steamer cruises by Cosens now continues and flourishes thanks to paddle steamers such as *Kingswear Castle*.